LISTENING IS *Healing*

LISTENING IS *Healing*

A Practical Guide for Pastoral Care

PETER MCINTOSH

authorHOUSE®

AuthorHouse™
1663 Liberty Drive
Bloomington, IN 47403
www.authorhouse.com
Phone: 1-800-839-8640

© 2013 by Peter McIntosh. All rights reserved.

No part of this book may be reproduced, stored in a retrieval system, or transmitted by any means without the written permission of the author.

Unless otherwise noted scripture quotations are taken from the King James Version (KJV) of the Bible—Public Domain.

Published by AuthorHouse   03/21/2013

ISBN: 978-1-4817-8696-6 (sc)
ISBN: 978-1-4817-8697-3 (e)

Any people depicted in stock imagery provided by Thinkstock are models, and such images are being used for illustrative purposes only.
Certain stock imagery © Thinkstock.

This book is printed on acid-free paper.

Because of the dynamic nature of the Internet, any web addresses or links contained in this book may have changed since publication and may no longer be valid. The views expressed in this work are solely those of the author and do not necessarily reflect the views of the publisher, and the publisher hereby disclaims any responsibility for them.

Contents

Preface vii

Chapter One:
    What Is a Listening Ministry? 1

Chapter Two:
    What Makes a Good Listener? 7

Chapter Three:
    A Dos and Don'ts Listening Checklist 20

Chapter Four:
    Listening for the Robbers 24

Chapter Five:
    Ministering into the Brokenness 61

Chapter Six:
    At the Conclusion of Ministry 105

Appendix: A Way Forward 109

Preface

Bear one another's burdens and so fulfil the law of Christ.

Galatians 6: 2

Bearing one another's burdens can take many forms. It can mean providing care through practical support or extending friendship to those in need, but it can also mean giving time to listen to people's stories when they want to talk.

Listening is healing, and a listening ministry can be a significant part of any care.

This book explains what a listening ministry can involve. It identifies who listeners might be. It provides insights into how to listen and what to listen for, and it describes how listeners can effectively respond to what they hear. It concludes with a practical guide for groups wishing to develop this ministry within their own church communities.

The church has a God-given mandate to care. A listening ministry is one way of fulfilling that caring "law of Christ".

Chapter One

What Is a Listening Ministry?

The thief cometh not, but for to steal, and to kill, and to destroy:

I am come that they might have life, and that they might have it more abundantly.

John 10: 10

My seven-year-old son was out playing on his bike on the concrete walkways surrounding our flat. When he returned, I was busy on my computer.

"Dad!" His voice was less strident than usual.

With my back to him I waved a gesture of "wait a minute".

"Dad," said the voice again, more urgently this time.

Still no response from me.

"Dad, I fell off my bike."

Again my irritated hand signalled at the interruption.

"Dad, I've hurt myself."

Without turning, I said with some irritancy, "Hang on, will you? I'm busy!"

I heard a sob, which was unlike him, so I glanced round, and to my horror I saw blood pouring down his face from what seemed like a hole in his head.

The rest of the scene was, to say the least, frenetic. An abandoned computer, a clutched son, a dash to the car, a racing drive to hospital, x-rays, stitches, and an almighty sigh of relief when appearances proved worse than reality. Only a superficial wound had occurred, and all would be well.

In the midst of the trauma he told me his story of the accident—how his head reached the concrete before the bike! Later, of course, he had another story to tell his friends, an impressive tale of blood, high-speed driving, hospitals, and undergoing what no doubt would be exaggerated into something major like brain surgery. Hopefully, he would omit the bit about the non-listening parent!

There are different kinds of listening. There is the listening we do when we are having an ordinary conversation with somebody, which (unless we are physically hard of hearing) is a listening we probably take for granted. Sometimes we are interested in what is being said to us, and sometimes we are not. Then there is the listening we do when we want to identify a particular sound like a kettle boiling, a baby crying, or the car engine playing up. However when it comes to a *listening ministry*, it is yet another kind of listening that takes place.

The word "ministry" can often put people off because of the belief that such work can only be done by professionals or those highly trained in every aspect of counselling or theology. However, if we think of ministry as exercising wise and compassionate care towards others, guided and inspired by the Holy Spirit, then such a work is potentially open to all who are gifted for it.

A listening ministry might be described as intentional listening, that is, listening to what is behind what the person is saying. Listeners then become like detectives; they listen to the story being told to them, but they also listen for the clues that point to what it is that is robbing the storyteller of peace and well-being. They listen for the feelings, emotions, and attitudes that accompany the story. They listen for how the person is inside in mind, heart, or spirit as he or she shares.

This may sound difficult, yet being a listening detective is probably not as far removed from our experience as we might imagine. Without realising it, we have probably all been effective detectives at some time or another. People can say something to us, and we know instinctively they mean something else. Here is an example: you have asked someone, "How are you?" and the person has responded, "Oh, can't complain," but you know their condition or their circumstances are such that they would complain if given permission. When somebody says, "I don't mind," you can tell when it's just a conventional way of being polite! When you hear the common ready response "I'm fine," you often sense it might stand for "I'm **F**ed up, **I**nsecure, **N**eurotic, and **E**xhausted!"

There can be many reasons why people need someone to listen to them and someone to talk to. In the story of the Good Samaritan in Luke's Gospel, chapter 10.25-37, Jesus tells of someone lying at the roadside "half dead". This person, on his journey, has been "attacked, stripped, robbed, and abandoned." Eventually, after two others reject him and pass by, someone comes along who is moved to minister to him in a variety of ways. Through such ministry the half-dead individual is eventually restored back to a fullness of life.

People's life journeys can sometimes leave them feeling half dead. They can be attacked, stripped, and robbed in all sorts of ways, not necessarily physically, but emotionally, mentally, or spiritually through circumstances, accident, hurtful events, painful relationships, or abuse. They can be robbed of self-worth, appreciation, love, security, care, well-being, or affection. They can find themselves unable to cope with the after-effects of some dreadful experience

Peter McIntosh

or the loss of a loved one. They may have gone down wrong roads that seemed more exciting than their daily round, and this may have proved disastrous. Perhaps they have been confronted by circumstances they couldn't handle or have been unjustly treated by another.

To restore their well-being will require more than having a cosy chat, comforting though that might be. If deeply affected lives are to be renewed and restored to wholeness, it will require more than just listening to someone's stories. When someone walks with a limp because of a stone in his or her shoe, identifying the stone alone will not take away the limp. The stone needs to be removed.

This defines the need for a *listening ministry*. It is a listening care that is able to discern and identify robbers of Christ's peace and eradicate them from the person's life. This is why listening is healing.

Chapter Two

What Makes a Good Listener?

The Spirit will lead you into all truth.

John 16: 13

You can sense when people are not really listening to you. The look in their eyes, their attitude, and their responses all affirm or deny their interest in what you are saying to them. In the end, if they are not good listeners, you will not tell them your story or share yourself with them. It follows that to be an effective listener, the first rule is to be the kind of person who actually invites and encourages a story from a storyteller. The effective listener makes the storyteller want to share more deeply all the details.

Before going further, test your own qualifications for being a potential listener by considering the following questions. Give yourself marks out of five-five being a resounding yes, and one being a probable no! Add your score up. See how many you have accumulated out of a possible forty-five.

- Do people seem to talk freely and openly to me?

- Do people readily share confidences with me and tell me things they perhaps could not or would not tell others?

- Do I feel at ease when listening to other people's stories, without being either shocked or embarrassed or having the desire to gossip about them afterwards?

- Do I feel a sense of compassion no matter what people are telling me about, even if I think it might be their own fault?

- Can I relate to other people's situations or circumstances, even when they are quite different to my own?

- Can I listen without taking the burdens of other people into myself?

- Am I prepared to listen without wanting to interrupt with my own stories or experiences?

- Do I want to know more about listening and restoring wholeness to those who share their stories with me?

- Am I prepared to be open to the Holy Spirit to lead and direct my understanding of what is being said and what needs addressing?

If your answer to these questions has in the main been a four or five—even a qualified, hesitant three—then you might be well suited to a listening ministry.

"Dad, I've fallen off my bike" was not too difficult a story for my son to relate to me or for me to eventually make a correct response. However, telling another person the truth, the whole truth, and nothing but the truth about your life, your personal feelings, and your intimate experiences is not easy. If the storyteller feels the truth could open him or her up to rejection, punishment, ridicule, or blame, he or she will keep quiet. It is not that people deliberately hide the truth or tell lies, although this can happen if someone is too afraid or ashamed to admit the truth.

It would have been different if my son had previously been told not to go out on his bike, if he had stolen the bike, or if he should have been somewhere else in the first place. If any of these circumstances had been the case, then it might not have been easy for him to come indoors and tell me his story. Guilt, fear of punishment, fear of being found out, shame—any of these things could have prevented him from seeking help and finding ultimate healing. This is how it can be with those who need or want to tell their story. They can feel reticent in coming forward to talk about things about which they may be deeply ashamed or fearful. An effective listener needs to be a real encourager so that the robbers of peace in the storyteller can be revealed, no matter who or what they might be.

So what makes an effective listener? The good listener draws out the other's story with comments like "Go on, take your time," or "Tell me more about that," or "What happened next?" These comments all help the storyteller believe the listener is genuinely interested in what he or she is saying. This belief gives the storyteller the confidence to go further with the story and share the parts that are difficult to talk about. Sentiments like "I hated my parent," "I've had an affair," "I can't forgive so-and-so," or "I was abused" are not easily brought out into the open. This can be especially true in a church environment, which can sometimes be felt to be a judgmental or condemnatory community. Yet it is these kinds of truths that need to be revealed if healing is to be found. If someone says, "I have never ever told anybody that," then that is a sign that the Spirit is at work. A return to wholeness may be on its way.

The good listener doesn't break into any silences in the storyteller's recounting. Sometimes as people talk, they may fall silent. In their mind they can be searching for the right words or reliving some experience or event. Silences can be the Spirit at work, bringing to the person's mind something that needs remembering and bringing into the open. If after a while the silence goes on, it can be helpful to gently ask, "What are you thinking?" or even "What are you seeing?"

Confidentiality, of course, is a must. Nobody will say anything if they feel the one to whom they are speaking cannot be trusted. Listeners always keep complete confidence. They handle with respect and honour everything that is given to them. This, of course, raises the question of what to do if someone tells of a criminal act he or she has carried out. It helps if guidelines are set out before listening begins. This way the storyteller knows that if he or she tells of something that is a criminal offence, it will have to be reported. This can actually be what is needed for healing. Perhaps the storyteller wants to tell someone of his or her wrongdoing but has never had the courage until now. If the information is offered to a caring listener, the storyteller will know that someone will stand alongside him or her. This will enable the consequences of the storyteller's actions to be dealt with compassionately.

Of course, it is not words alone that tell what other people are thinking or feeling. The look on their faces, in their eyes, their body movements—these will all give an indication of what is going on inside. The aware listener watches for these things. The eyes are the windows of the soul. The look on another's face often provides a clue to the feelings behind the words. The way people sit or move, what is happening with their hands—all these things help the listener discern the truth of the Spirit within the storyteller. The opposite is also the case. Good listeners are careful about their own demeanour, their attire, their look. They need to ensure that nothing will detract from the storyteller's confidence in speaking to them.

The good listener always keeps one ear on the storyteller and the other ear open to God's spirit of wisdom and truth. To help listeners discern the truth within the story, the right question to ask can often come to mind prompted by the Holy Spirit. The Spirit's gift of *discernment* is key in this matter. It is something that a listener needs to pray for and be utterly dependent upon in this ministry.

To allow this gift of discernment to play its full part, listeners need to keep a variety of questions in their own mind while the other person is sharing with them. The following list contains some suitable examples.

- What impressions am I getting?
- What did that word or phrase mean?
- Do I need to ask more about what they have just revealed at this point?
- Do I need to ask them how they feel about this or that event or experience?
- Should I question what the truth is about what they have just said?
- Should I keep quiet?
- Is there a passage of scripture or a picture coming into my mind?
- Do I need to stop them at this point?

Listening is best done in pairs. It might seem intimidating for the storyteller to be faced with two people, but it can be done in a sensitive way. To avoid making the storyteller feel uncomfortable, he or she can be offered the choice of where to sit. Only one of the pair of listeners should take the lead while the other remains mostly silent. The silent partner can be praying inwardly. This partner will perhaps hear something the other has missed and can interject as and when appropriate.

There may be some value in offering people this ministry after a regular church service. Nevertheless, it is something best done by appointment at a specific place and time that is conducive to stories being told and ministry being received. It takes quality time to listen to someone in depth. It is no use expecting people to reveal their innermost secrets in a hurried or snatched conversation on a street corner, in a bus queue, or at a chance meeting. Even if they do blurt out an event or experience, the intentional listener will make sure to set aside *intentional time* for the storyteller. Listeners need to provide a proper environment, one in which they can hear what is being said for as long as it takes and in which can offer appropriate ministry.

The best way for this to happen is to arrange to meet at a mutually acceptable time. There needs to be agreement about the length of time to be shared. It is not helpful if the storyteller does not know how much time he or she has. The conversation can ramble. More importantly, storytellers can keep hedging away from the real truth that they want to share. If they know there are only a few minutes left, then they just might risk telling what is at the heart of their concern. They will do this more readily if they know they can escape after having taken the plunge to speak it out. This means that it helps if each party knows the timetable. If the time needs to be extended and it is convenient, then of course agreement can be reached to do so. There needs to be no pressure on listener or storyteller. It may be better to share for an hour and return another day than to try to listen to too much all at once. In this, as in all things, there is a need for the listener to be open to the Spirit's leading.

Listening is not a ministry for those who cannot or do not wish to get alongside others. Compassionate listeners need to be able to sense something of what it's like to be in storyteller's shoes. They need to appreciate where any tears come from and not be afraid of them. It is not sympathy that is required but empathy. This is not a ministry for those who simply want to *do* something to other people in a dominant or holier-than-thou sort of way.

Listening is Healing

Compassion and sensitivity towards people of all kinds and persuasions are a must. A comprehensive listening ministry cannot choose to whom it will listen. All genders, creeds, nationalities, and social types must know themselves to be welcome without fear of exclusion. For some listeners, this might be a difficult proposition with which to be faced; they may have natural and moral inclinations towards some people more than others. These sensitivities have to be put aside if everybody is to be able to find a listening ear without exclusion.

Of course, some might question the point of listening. You cannot change the way people are. They have always been like that. There is nothing you can do about it. They will never get over it.

From a potential storyteller's point of view, this hopelessness is understandable. A painful experience may have led to disillusionment or a feeling that nothing will ever come right again. Listeners themselves, hearing so many stories of hurt, pain, and human failing, need to hold fast to their own beliefs. They need to trust that this is a ministry of resurrection that does enable people to discover new life. The good listener is one who has a firm and mature faith in God's promises to ransom, heal, restore, and forgive.

All this may sound somewhat daunting. You might feel that this is a job only for the skilled counsellor or highly trained expert. You might feel that this is not for the church community. People do spend a great deal of time and money in seeking help from professional agencies, but they are also happy to go to less than professional sources for succour. When people are desperately hungry or thirsty, they will eat or drink whatever is on offer and will not question whether it is wholesome or based on sound principles. Drowning men and women do grasp at straws. So do those in deep emotional or spiritual need. If the church does not offer succour, then other less healing or less wholesome sources will, moving people further from God's love and grace.

This does not mean that being engaged in a listening ministry is a work for the well-meaning amateur or misguided enthusiast. This is not a work for those who want to counsel others to

Listening is Healing

meet their own emotional needs or personal ambitions. An effective listener needs to be the kind of person who is willing to develop the necessary gifts and skills needed for such ministry. Above all they need to be open to the Holy Spirit, confident they will be given all that is needful to fulfil this ministry. This confidence stems from the belief that it is Christ who seeks the well-being of others, and therefore He will equip His church and its people for the task.

Chapter Three

A Dos and Don'ts Listening Checklist

- Before meeting with the storyteller, pray for discernment, wisdom, and protection.

- If there are two of you listening, agree beforehand who will take the main lead.

- Pray for the person that he or she may be open to the Spirit's prompting.

- Make sure the listening environment is peaceful.

- Switch off the phone, the family, and the front door.

- Let the storyteller decide where to sit.

- Start with something simple like "What have you done today?" or "How did you get here?"

- Help the storyteller relax so that you are relaxed when you meet.

Listening is Healing

- Make sure the storyteller knows how long your time together can be.

- Reassure the storyteller that whatever is said will not be repeated anywhere else unless it is of a criminal nature, and even then it will be dealt with in a sensitive way.

- Begin with prayer, inviting the Holy Spirit to lead you into all truth and giving thanks for the presence of the risen Christ with you.

- Ask them where they would like to begin, and assure them they can start wherever they want.

- Have a box of tissues on hand.

- Let tears flow. Do not stop them, but rather, encourage them.

- Let them be silent, if they want to be.

- Let any silence go on; don't you break it first.

- Don't supply them with words. Let them find their own.

- Watch their eyes, their face, and their body movements.
- Listen to the tone of voice, as well as the words.
- Check what their descriptive words mean—for example, when they say, "It was awful," or "I felt devastated," or "I was hurt."
- Ask them what, who, why, where, when—if it helps the story go deeper.
- Never give advice. Instead, ask what they would do, or say, or prefer.
- Have a Bible handy, but don't keep thumbing through it while you are listening.
- After an hour of listening, consider letting ministry take over.
- Arrange to meet again if appropriate.
- When they have gone, jot down anything needed for a future meeting.

- Hand them over to God; let it be; don't talk about them.

- Let go, and let God.

Chapter Four

Listening for the Robbers

> *And Jesus answering said, A certain man went down from Jerusalem to Jericho, and fell among thieves, which stripped him of his raiment, and wounded him, and departed, leaving him half dead.*
>
> Luke 10: 30-37

For what are listeners listening? In a listening ministry, when people sit and talk, it's not just their story or their experiences that matter but also how these things might have affected them. Listeners are trying to discern in what ways people may have been robbed of peace during their life journey.

So what robs people of wholeness? What makes life for some little more than a journey of quiet despair? Who or what can leave them half dead emotionally, physically, or spiritually? What hinders them experiencing fullness of life and well-being?

Robbers of wholeness can be identified. There need be no great secret or mystique about them. They can be classed as follows.

1. Hurts
2. Sins
3. Chains
4. Occult

These are the four major robbers of fullness of life in Christ. These are the attackers of wholeness, and it is these that listeners look out for when someone wants to share his or her story with them. These are the disturbers that the effective listener seeks to identify and address.

Listeners can learn to recognise these robbers and distinguish their hallmarks. They can learn to discern their presence when people share their life experiences with them. However it is not the listener who then has to deal with them.

This is Christ's ministry, which the listener simply enables.

1. Listening for the Hurts.

In recent years we have become much more familiar with what makes people the way they are. The fields of psychology and psychoanalysis have given us considerable insights and understandings. A friend of mine has a wooden bowl carved out of the root of a very old olive tree. The bowl shows all the blemishes and indentations which the years of growth, drought, stones, and damage have wrought upon the wood or, to put it another way, all the wounds which that tree had experienced. When listeners are listening for human *hurts*, they are really listening for the wounds caused by these hurts to determine what needs Christ's healing touch.

The story of the Good Samaritan recorded in Luke's Gospel is the parable of a man on a journey. On that journey he is attacked. We are told that he is robbed, stripped, beaten up, passed by, and left half dead at the roadside. Imagine what this man might feel as he slowly recovers from the attack before the healing

Samaritan reaches him. Surely there will be anger, bitterness, resentment, disillusionment, and despair. He will have feelings of rejection, abandonment, and perhaps even guilt over having taken the road he took. He will know he has been abused. These powerful emotions would certainly have robbed him of any peace or wholeness in his years ahead had he not received the ministry he did. Filled with vitriol, he would have told his story of the attack many times to any who would listen. Flogging and hanging would be his view of justice. He would view priests and religion with scorn and cynicism. His own thoughts about himself might well turn to ones of self-loathing at what had been done to him. He would see himself as a victim, with self-pity a constant companion within. Telling his story to others would not help if his hearers were not equipped to identify the unseen robbers of peace within him and did not know how to deal with them.

Of course this is a parable, but it offers a clear example of the need to minister to wounds inflicted by hurts. Hurts are common robbers of well-being. They can attack people at any time in all sorts of ways and circumstances, small and large. They can powerfully influence the way people are. They can determine how people feel about themselves or about others. They can sway how they feel about God or life itself.

When listening to someone's story, it is often the hurts which can be discerned first. The clues to wounds inflicted by hurts can usually be detected by tell-tale attitudes. Bitterness, resentment, and anger will be in evidence. A lack of self-worth, feelings of not belonging or being easily rejected, and a need for constant reassurance would be among the more obvious signs displayed by the storyteller.

Stories of rejection, loss, disappointment, or abuse can often relate to womb, infant, childhood, or teenage experiences. Listeners need to be aware that these formative years are highly sensitive. They are vulnerable times of life, when hurts can easily take place. These hurts can result in damaged emotions years after they are first experienced, preventing wholeness in adult life. There was a storyteller who could never bear to wear necklaces or scarves around her neck. She discovered in later life that at

Listening is Healing

her birth the umbilical cord had wrapped itself around her neck, nearly choking the life from her as she was being born. Although she had no conscious memory of this, that early physical hurt influenced her whole life in the way she dressed.

How do listeners discern the root cause of wounding? How do they determine what it is that has caused some obvious distress in the other? It can be helpful for listeners to put together a picture of their storyteller's early years. Could any hurt then have been the source of any disquiet now? To create this picture, the listener might need to ask directly or indirectly questions such as the following.

- When, where, and how was life for the storyteller's mother during pregnancy? Was it a peaceful, happy situation?

- Who made up the family at birth? Did they have brothers and sisters? Were they the youngest or oldest? Were they accepted by their siblings?

- Did they accept siblings born after them or was there jealousy?

- Were they a "mistake", an "accident", or the wrong gender (parents wanting a girl when they were a boy or hoping for a boy when they turned out to be a girl)?

- Were they an only child and therefore used to constant attention?

- Were they robbed of any security, attention, or love through some event or situation in their early years?

- Did they have to face deprived or stressful circumstances, such as the death of a parent or sibling, when they were young?

- Was there a divorce, separation, or adoption within their family?

- Were they adopted, fostered, or sent away to school?

- Were they spoilt, belittled, put down, abused, not allowed to make mistakes, or not permitted to do things for themselves as they were growing up?

The answers to these questions may or may not point to hurts that occurred, but they may provide clues to the storyteller's disquiet now. Hurts can come at any time, any moment in life. Just because people are adult in years or mature in outlook, it does not necessarily mean they are going to be free from attack. Hurts are part and parcel of life and living. Robbers of well-being exist at every turn, even if they don't manage to steal on every occasion. The listener should be aware of the possible circumstances that can rob the person. These would include the following.

- The death of a spouse, or some close friend
- Divorce or separation
- An offspring's marriage
- Being fired from work, demoted, or having to face some business adjustment
- A change in home conditions or a move to a new environment
- A change in financial state or financial responsibility
- Sexual difficulties or related bad experiences

- Ill health
- A brush with the law
- Being falsely accused or misunderstood
- A change in lifestyle or usual routines and habits

Of course, what wounds one person may not wound another. How one person reacts to the same set of circumstances or life experiences may be quite different from another's response. Listeners listening to events being related listen for what affect these events may have had, but they need to take great care not to jump to conclusions. "Never make assumptions" should be written large on the walls of any place in which they are listening to someone's story.

It may be that storytellers are painfully aware of their own hurts. They might simply tell about them without the need for any great detective skills on the listener's part. They might describe an incident or share a happening in their infancy, childhood, teenage years, or later life that clearly caused them deep hurt. They have no problem in remembering, even if they feel they cannot do anything about the way it has affected them. However, it could be that something that seems to have hurt them out of all proportion is actually an indication of a much deeper hurt in the past. In other words, what is being heard may not be the real problem.

An example of this is the story of a mother asking if she could talk to someone about her only son going off to university. She said that while she was glad for him to be going there, she was very anxious about it herself. The listener, sensing more than a natural concern about an offspring leaving home, checked for more clues. He gently asked her how her husband felt. Her response was to say he didn't care in the same way she did. The tone of her voice was quite dismissive of him. Again the listener gently probed by asking how supportive he was to her concern. Eventually the whole story poured out. She and her husband now had little or no relationship. She was dreading being at home with him alone without her son. She did not feel she could cope. He had had an affair many years previously, and she had never forgiven him. She could only live with the knowledge as long as there was a threesome at home with the son. Now the truth was out. It was not the son leaving that was the robber of peace; it was the broken unresolved hurt from the husband. It was in that area that appropriate ministry was needed.

Sometimes storytellers will not or cannot speak about the hurts they have experienced. They might be ashamed of how they feel, or they may want to protect somebody like a parent or a loved one. They could be hiding a secret relationship. They might want to keep up the pretence that there is nothing wrong in life, afraid to admit they cannot cope. They might be ashamed to own up to what they believe to be worthless failings. They might feel they ought to be overcoming things with their own strength; they should not be letting down their faith by being un-Christian in some way, through not being able to snap out of such unworthy feelings, as they see them. Fear and pride are great blocks to admitting truth about yourself or your life. Listeners always need to be sensitive, compassionate encouragers in teasing out the truth that will uncover the hurts. But gentle

Listening is Healing

probing has to be the method. Listeners have no right to go into areas with which the storyteller cannot cope. It can be too painful. No dentist would dig deep into the decaying tooth without appropriate anaesthetic.

Listeners also need to remember that even if they personally feel the storyteller's hurt is of no consequence, perhaps even trivial, if the storyteller has been wounded by it, then that *is* what matters. It is not helpful to say to someone, "You shouldn't feel like that," if in fact they do. It shows the listener is not really hearing them.

Sometimes people are unaware of the cause of their wounds, although their effect might clearly be taking its toll. They may be unhappy, disturbed, or depressed, yet have no idea what the reasons are. They have settled for an "It's just the way I am!" philosophy. In this case the listener searches for clues among their life experiences, seeking for what needs to be addressed. It is similar to a doctor listening to the symptoms before diagnosing the cause of the malady.

Put simply, deep-rooted hurts can wound body, mind, or spirit. Untreated wounds can cause a dis-ease that robs people of fullness of life in Christ. By means of a listening ministry, under the guidance of the Holy Spirit, He would seek to seal and heal their wounds once and for all.

2. Listening for the Sins.

> *The Son of Man has authority on earth to forgive sins*
>
> Mark 2: 10

Guilt has a powerful influence on people's lives. It is a cancerous robber of health and well-being. It can paralyse, depress, and damage body, mind, spirit, and relationships, and listeners may discern it in the stories told to them.

Guilt stems from people believing they have done something wrong against whomever (or whatever) they feel or believe to be the ultimate judge of their life, God or not God. It takes root when they believe they cannot be forgiven or do not deserve to be forgiven, or they feel they have become totally unacceptable to their ultimate judge. In other words, they are beyond redemption!

This sense of guilt can have many roots. These include heavy-handed, moralistic parenting, imposed religious beliefs centred on judgement and punishment, and belonging to criticising communities that demand you achieve acceptability because love is seen as something that is conditional.

It could be that the storyteller has only known conditional love, the kind fostered by promises that you will be loved, rewarded, accepted, or appreciated if, or when, or as long as, and so on. "Santa will bring you a present *if* you have been good." This attitude, often imposed in the vulnerable formative years, results in people feeling that they have never been worthy enough to be loved, let alone worthy to receive forgiveness. The result is that they may never have been free from a sense of guilt or a loss of self-worth.

It would not be difficult when talking about sin to get into a lengthy, complicated debate about its nature, origins, and theological and doctrinal concepts. What the listener *means* by sin does not matter as much as what their storyteller *feels* about it. If the storyteller believes things he or she has done, said, or been have been sins against their rule-maker, law-giver, or judge, then guilt will not be far away and his or her wholeness will be under threat.

Listeners may need to help storytellers question their own definition of sin and their own grounds of belief, since it is their ideas about sin that will determine their feelings about it. This may not be an easy task for the listener. Our natural inclination is to project our own beliefs and value judgements onto others. For example, if the listener believes that women should wear hats in church, but the storyteller does not feel it matters significantly, then the listener must accept that is where the storyteller is rather than try to impose his or her own judgement. Such an imposition would only lead the storyteller to be more burdened by guilt—the very thing from which he or she is seeking release.

Therefore, instead of entering into an arid debate about the nature and cause of sin or projecting their own concepts of it, listeners need to discern whether storytellers have committed sins according to their *own* dictates.

If the listener detects an excessive need for constant self-justification, it might be a clue that guilt may be at the heart of the storyteller's problem. Criticising others, handing out blame and condemnation, or repeated claims that people are not good enough to receive approval would be indicators. The listener must watch for these things and check out the stories to see if the reasons for this sense of guilt can be identified.

Disabling emotions may also arise from the sins the storyteller feels have been committed against him or her. The listener listens for people in the storytellers' tales whom they cannot or will not forgive. This lack of forgiveness can be directed towards any of three sources—themselves, others, or God. Such an unforgiving spirit might have generated within them a powerful sense of bitterness or deep-seated resentment.

The listener will soon be able to discern an unforgiving spirit in the heart or mind of the storyteller. Attitudes, tone of voice, and way of speaking about themselves, others, or God will clearly demonstrate the existence of this powerful destructive robber of wholeness.

In the story of the paralysed man recorded in the Gospels of Matthew, Mark, and Luke, we are told of someone with a physical condition, whose friends bring him to Jesus for cure. What is significant is what affects the cure. "You are forgiven," Jesus pronounces over the man. The effect of this pronouncement is startling. The paralysis falls away. Not only does the man take up his bed, he runs, no doubt terrified at what has happened and being the centre of such attention. It was not some magic touch that brought release to the man; it was the power of being forgiven. Knowing he was forgiven made the difference. Jesus clearly discerned that guilt was at the root of the man's condition. We are not told what the guilt was or what sins he had committed or felt he had committed. We are just told that it was forgiveness that brought about the change. Of course, argument followed. Only God could forgive, so who was this Jesus who felt He could proclaim it?

Listening is Healing

The relevance of this event to any listening ministry is the power of guilt to rob people of wholeness and the power of forgiveness to heal. The listener to any story needs to be aware that there is a difference between "I *won't* forgive" and "I *can't* forgive." The former indicates a hurting desire for revenge on the part of storytellers, getting their own back on those who have hurt or harmed them in the past. The latter is a cry for help, recognition that even though they are willing to forgive and want to let go of ill-harboured thoughts, they cannot. This difference is important, because it will ultimately determine the different ministry that needs to be exercised by listeners.

Another question related to sin and sinning arises. What if the storyteller doesn't acknowledge any error or wrongdoing? What if they are clearly involved in some criminal activity or in socially abnormal behavioural practices? What should be the response of the listening detective then? The law requires listeners to pass on information that is revealed to them about abuse, terrorism, or other criminal acts.

The listener needs to ensure that the storyteller knows this before any story is related.

The listener can question the attitudes and behaviour of the other but in the end must leave the final choices the storyteller is prepared to make about his or her own life to the storyteller. This can be hard, especially when you want the best for others and feel their choices may not be in their best interests or even Spirit-led. But the fact of the matter is that listeners cannot live other people's lives for them. True healing comes when storytellers seek to make right decisions and choices for themselves.

Sins committed against the storyteller, sins committed by the storyteller, and sins the storyteller has not recognised or acknowledge are robbers of peace, well-being, and wholeness. The listener watches and listens with non-judgemental compassion, care, and humility. As we shall see, once identified and brought into the light, they can then be addressed in ways that bring release and newness of life.

3. Listening for the Chains

> *Stand fast therefore in the liberty wherewith Christ hath made us free, and be not entangled again with the yoke of bondage.*
>
> Galatians 5: 1

The next robber of well-being and wholeness could be described as the *chain gang*. Chains restrict, limit, inhibit, and enslave. The listener is on the lookout for evidence of this in the storyteller's life. Virtually anything can enslave people—*habits, beliefs, ideas, people, places, or possessions*. These can influence people in ways that prevent them having freedom of will or choice. They can exercise a power over their thinking, behaviour, attitudes, and decisions. People become less than whole when they are not free agents in control of their own bodies, minds, and spirits. The chains that bind people enslave people. It is these chains that the listener seeks to identify so they can be addressed and broken.

Damaging *habits* are the most obvious restrictors of freedom. If the storyteller showed signs of addictions to smoking, drinking, excessive eating, pornography, or drugs, these could be seen as chains that might be potential damagers to health and wholeness. However there is a difference between a destructive habit and simple self-indulgence. As always, the listener should be careful not to make wrong assumptions just because their storyteller indicates he or she occasionally smokes or likes the odd glass of sherry!

If persons are enslaved by habit, they are not free. They cannot choose to indulge or abstain. Such bondage can not only damage life but can dictate a way of living. Revealed habits could be considered by listeners as an outward sign of some more deep-rooted hurt or problem. It might be this that would require attention if the storyteller wished to be free and regain control over his or her own life.

There are also less obvious chains than habits. *Beliefs and ideas* can enslave. There is a proverb which gives a clue here. "Be careful how you think; your life is shaped by your thoughts." What people believe about themselves can enslave them in a harmful way, especially if what they believe is negative, self-destructive, or actually untrue.

In story-telling the listener listens out for self-cursing as an indicator of low self-esteem—phrases like "I am no use," "I'm hopeless," or "I'm not very good." The question is who told them this? Where did they learn this view of themselves? People can often influence how others feel about themselves. There is nothing wrong in that if what has been said has encouraged, supported, or built the person up in a wholesome way. "Darling, I think you're wonderful" can be very affirming. However, those who have had less than affectionate attitudes directed towards them might well have formulated beliefs and ideas about themselves which produce a low self-esteem. Listeners watch out for this within the storyteller. They seek to discover from whence such negativity originated. It could have been that cross or angry words were spoken powerfully against the storyteller at a vulnerable time, words that still enslave his or her thinking long after the time of their speaking or shouting. For example, an irritated or pressurised teacher might have said to them, "You're stupid. You can't do anything right!" This common enough outburst might well have gone deep enough in that moment for it to have taken root within them so that from then on they actually believed it to be true. "You're ugly, too tall, too short, too fat, too thin!" Again, these are words which can stay to chain people to the false belief that they are unacceptable or unattractive. They end up living in bondage to what others have said to them in the past.

Such bondage to distorted beliefs about oneself is not the only chain that can influence and inhibit inner feelings. Distorted religious beliefs can also detrimentally enslave and dictate a way of life. Erroneous, destructive beliefs about the nature of God, for example, can rob people of a healthy faith or a mature spirituality. They may have suffered a strict religious upbringing from home or church. God may have been viewed as a judgemental, punitive, and legalistic figure. A storyteller was asked to imagine the look on the face of Jesus when He looked at her. "Utter disgust" was her immediate reply. It was an image that needed changing. People may have been taught that God's grace and love must be earned, achieved, or awarded rather than received openly and unconditionally. The woman caught in adultery in the biblical account recorded in John's Gospel was not judged by Jesus according to the religious law of the day. Instead, she found His mercy given unconditionally, before He encouraged her to change her life style.

Distorted or inhibiting religious beliefs would be something the listener looks out for to see if there is any dis-ease within the storyteller related to an inhibiting religiosity of any kind. Of course, this does not mean listeners belittle or pour scorn on another's seriously held convictions of faith. What they are looking for is the person in bondage to an idea or tenet of faith that is robbing them of being fully human or even fully divine, a belief preventing them from having healthy relationship with their God.

Being in bondage to distorted beliefs is perhaps more easily understood than being enslaved by a *relationship*. Bonding between people is a healthy part of anyone's story. Being in bondage to them is not. The storyteller might be enslaved by another. This could be a relationship that prevents the storyteller from being free to be him—or herself, to run his or her own life, or to make his or her own decisions. It could be an inhibiting chain that exists between the storyteller and the one who has hold over him or her mentally, emotionally, or even physically. This chain, which will have been forged at some point in the storyteller's life, binds in ways that restrict or disable. In the end, the storyteller might even choose to be a victim or feel that there is no choice other than to be a doormat on which people wipe their feet.

This bondage to another can even mean being enslaved by someone who has died. This would show itself by storytellers indicating their routines, practices, or habits were influenced by what they felt were the desired wishes of a deceased partner, parent, or other relationship.

Stephen never married and lived with his mother for over twenty years. When she died, she was buried in a cemetery some distance from where they had lived. Every Sunday without fail, rain, hail, or shine, Stephen would go to her graveside and spend time there. He never missed. He would never take a holiday or go away for a weekend, thinking he would be letting his mother down if he did so. Talking about this with an understanding listener, he was asked, "Did your mother every visit that cemetery when she was alive?"

When he thought about it, Stephen admitted she had never been there.

"Then why go to a place she never knew? Can she not be in your heart wherever you are?" It took Stephen many months to break himself of the slavish routine and discover a fullness of life once again.

The chain that links the living with the dead can be a strong one, forged out of unresolved grief or fear. The listener would need to sensitively question the storyteller about the nature of the relationship that had existed during the other person's lifetime. Had the storyteller been able to grieve? Were covenants made, such as "I promise you I will never remarry" or "I'll never sell our house"? Is the storyteller now tied to these covenants emotionally even against his or her own desires through changing circumstances perhaps years later.

To see more clearly how this particular chain was forged and how it might be broken in a releasing and sensitive way could be part of the ministry required. Jesus made no covenants with His nearest and dearest. "It is to your advantage that I go" was His word to them.

Being in bondage to another person is not an easy chain to discern or unravel in another's story. There is a fine line between someone taking proper responsibility for someone else, perhaps a sick relative, a housebound parent or the like, and being in bondage to them. There is always a narrow margin between loving another and possessing another, between being loved by them and being possessed by them.

Sometimes these relationships are hidden. The storyteller does not want anybody to know of a secret love or union. This is why confidentiality matters so much. If people are to tell their story as it is, with no pretence, they must have confidence in the listener's ability not to be shocked or condemnatory. They must be able to trust the listener will not disclose the information that is passed on. If the hidden relationship proves to be destructive or damaging, that will

Listening is Healing

come out it in the telling about it. The listener can then help the storyteller evaluate his or her choices and possible courses of action. Moralising is not helpful or healing; it simply adds to the guilt. The storyteller with any sense will walk away, and the phrase "listening is healing" will mean nothing.

Bondage to *places* is another chain the listener should bear in mind as something that might be causing an unhealthy disquiet in the other. This would be recognised when storytellers indicate that a particular place seems to have some kind of hold on them or seems in some way to be essential to their well-being. They might speak of a place, such as a house, or an area they could not leave under any circumstances, a place which dictated their decisions related to their life and living. The storyteller may give reasons for being in such bondage to a particular place, and the listener would want to check if this was just the natural human predilection for somewhere to call home or a chain which was enslaving the individual beyond reasonable boundaries.

Bondage to *possessions* similarly needs to be recognised. People have favourite belongings, mementoes, and keepsakes. They have items which are precious to them, things they hold dear for all sorts of romantic or sentimental reasons. However, if possessing something takes hold in such a way that a person cannot live without it and cannot let it go if the need arises, then he or she has to consider if he or she is being possessed by this thing. Listeners might want to hear whether there are any possessions in the storytellers' lives that mean so much to them that they could not be without them, things that have enslaved them beyond reasonable limits rather than things that simply give them wholesome enjoyment. Any material possession that can govern behaviour or outlook becomes suspect, including *money*.

It is said, "The love of money is the root of all evil." Listeners might want to observe the storytellers' attitudes towards money. Can they not get enough of it, not spend it, and not give it? Do they associate value or status with having it? People can actually be in bondage to the need for having money, not as a normal means of economic living, but as a sign and symbol of personal standing and worth. They can have an inability to give it or spend it, not because they are mean or greedy, but because they see it as a measure of their worth.

People can also be in bondage to status or standing. When people retire and lose a position they once held, this can sometimes lead to depression and loss of self-worth. They might have been happy to retire and give up the daily round. They might have been made to retire for some reason. If their self-worth relied on what they did or who they were, disquiet can soon take hold. The listener must be sensitive to this circumstance in the storyteller's life.

Healing comes when people recognise that their worth and value is not dependent upon possessions, wealth, or status but upon being utterly acceptable to God just as they are. When a new-born baby comes into the world in the right circumstances, it is valued, appreciated, adored, and accepted, despite the fact that it has done nothing, achieved nothing, said nothing, and created nothing. Self-worth comes not from what we possess or from social standing or education or wealth. It comes from knowing ourselves to be a child of God.

The lesson for listeners is that *anything* and *anybody* can enslave and be part of a chain gang. That being the case, they must listen with care to what is going on behind the stories they are being told to discern if any freedom which Christ promises has been restricted or taken away.

4. Listening for the Occult

> *For we wrestle not against flesh and blood, but against principalities, against powers, against the rulers of the darkness of this world, against spiritual wickedness in high places.*
>
> Ephesians 6: 12

Attitudes towards the occult can range from scepticism to obsession. People can look on the subject with anything from idle curiosity to extreme fascination. Within the church it can be brought to the fore or simply overlooked. In circumstances like this, it is little wonder listeners need to be enlightened, aware, and prepared.

Listening is Healing

Unfortunately, the subject is often portrayed either sensationally or with a belittling ridicule. Powerful and widely accessible media of many kinds often give the occult and demonic a grossly distorted image that is far from its true nature and content. It therefore becomes a subject whose power to rob people of wholeness is easily dismissed by those who would believe themselves to be mature and level-headed in such matters. Sadly, this distortion only serves to disguise the reality of the power of potential occult influence that is readily available in ordinary situations of everyday life. The word "occult" actually means *hidden*, and it this hidden enemy of wholeness that listeners seek to bring to light if necessary as they hear the person's story.

Like the other robbers, this subject is one which requires wisdom and discernment to unravel from within stories. Listeners need to be able to recognise the variety of occult practices, which can range from an inclination to folklore or superstition on the one hand to satanic or demonic possession on the other. The listener also needs to differentiate between the damage caused by occult involvement and that caused by the hurts, sins, or chains documented previously. In other words, the sensitive listener needs to discern the difference between the power of evil and the power of human emotion and natural response.

One way of viewing the occult is to think of it as *spiritual adultery*. Rather than staying faithful to the one true God revealed in Jesus, people go elsewhere for succour, help, guidance, comfort, and even healing. They invite influences other than the influence of God's Holy Spirit to have control over their lives.

Listeners can recognise indicators of spiritual adultery when storytellers talk, for example, about their star sign or a lucky colour or number or refer readily to luck itself. The phrase "That was lucky" is often used in common parlance, giving credit for blessings to luck rather than to God. People often say "Touch wood" when looking for protection or the avoidance of ill fortune. Storytellers may have had their palm read or looked at their horoscope or even gone to a spiritualist meeting for solace or guidance.

Ignorance about occult influence can prevent the storyteller from even mentioning these things as part of his or her life experience. Storytellers may have been involved in spiritual adultery, but they would not know or believe it to be a potential source of harm. They would consider such things as only "a bit of fun" and not as something to be taken seriously. This is a weak argument against being robbed of peace or well-being. The child may go the medicine cupboard just for a bit of fun and take a pill to eat, thinking it to be a harmless sweet. The child's ignorance or lack of intention will sadly not detract from any harm the pill might cause. People can drink impure water without being aware that it contains harmful substances and still be infected. Not believing there is harm is no protection from being robbed of well-being.

What then does the listener listen for specifically that would indicate possible involvement with the occult? What are the signs that spiritual adultery may have taken place? What are the clues?

Perhaps the easiest way of answering this is to list some of the more obvious areas that relate to common occult practice which listeners might come across in any storyteller's account. These harmful influences can be entered into either through ignorance, or they can be sought after by deliberate choice.

- Astrology, horoscopes, and star signs
- Clairvoyance, fortune telling, and palmistry
- Mediums, spiritualists, and mysticism
- Palmistry, tea leaves, second sight, and tarot cards
- Lucky charms and lucky numbers
- The Ouija board
- Dungeons and Dragons
- Witches, covens, and black or white magic
- Voodoo
- Superstitions
- Transcendental meditation, telepathy, and séances

- New Age healing
- Preoccupation with the paranormal or spirit world
- Necromancy
- Books, videos, games, DVDs, and films specialising in the occult or demonic

Of course, the fact that storytellers might refer to having a part in any of these things does not necessarily mean they have become influenced or damaged by them. It is true to say that some people seem more susceptible to occult influence than others. You can walk across a minefield without being injured or killed, even though the mines are real enough.

As in other areas of detection, assumptions need to be checked and double checked to avoid wrongly attributing damage to the power of evil. The true cause of the storyteller's brokenness might well stem from other quarters. Listeners have to be discerning when confronted with evidence of involvement in occult practice in order to be able to determine the effect, if any, it has had on the storyteller's life.

Balance is essential so that the seriousness of the occult is neither underestimated nor over-emphasised. Listeners need to learn and understand without themselves becoming obsessed by the subject over and above all other aspects related to the listening ministry. Storytellers are done no favours if listeners believe that the demonic is present at every turn and place in the stories they hear, just as they would do storytellers no favours if they were to reject the reality of its presence at all.

Jesus encouraged His people to pray "and deliver us from evil" on every occasion, and He knew the reason why.

Chapter Five

Ministering into the Brokenness

I sought the Lord, and he heard me, and delivered me from all my fears

Psalm 34: 4

Now that the stones in the limping storyteller's shoe have been identified, they need to be removed. However, it is not the listener who heals the sick, binds the wounds, or releases the captives from their emotional or spiritual prisons. The listener is the enabler. The listener enables the storyteller to hand over any destructive elements within his or her story. It is God who redeems them. The listener cannot forgive, but God can. The listener cannot heal the wounds, but God can. The listener cannot remove the disturbing memory, but God can. The listener cannot bring them from their dark place into light, but God can.

Christian prayer is at the heart of the listening ministry. After listening to the storytellers, praying with them and encouraging them to pray are the powerful means through which change and renewal take place.

Prayer has a range of emphasis and styles that includes thanksgiving, confession, intercession, and petition. Through these different kinds of prayer, the storyteller has a variety of redeeming possibilities for healing. The variety allows specific kinds of prayer to address the particular kind of experiences the storyteller has shared. The Good Samaritan used a variety of ways and means to restore the man at the roadside. His ministry included bandages, oil, wine, a donkey, an inn, an innkeeper, money, and assurances. Listeners too have a variety of prayers and resources at their disposal as they minister to the storyteller's need. The ways in which they are used will depend on the character and beliefs of the storyteller and the causes of his or her brokenness. Their use will also depend on the gifts and spirituality of the listener. Each situation will be different because people are different. The common factor is the ministry

Listening is Healing

of the Holy Spirit at work in both listener and storyteller alike.

Prayer ministry is not simply engaging in a rigid set pattern of prayer. It is a precious time when listeners and storytellers alike are open to God's Spirit at work among them. Although different kinds of prayer have been outlined below, they are not something which the listener simply goes through automatically. The Holy Spirit may have other ideas as to what is needed. The prayers listed are indicators of the ways in which the Spirit might prompt or lead. Every person being different, their differences are honoured by God.

It may be appropriate in any prayer time to accompany prayer with the traditional laying on of hands. This action has a sound biblical and ecclesiastical background. It simply means that the listener stands over the kneeling or seated storyteller and places the hands lightly on or just above the recipient's head while offering prayer. It emphasises blessing and mirrors Christ's own ministry to some of those who came to Him. By this act, the storyteller can become more powerfully aware of the Holy Spirit at work in the healing. However, listeners should never take such action without the full consent of the storyteller, even when listeners feel it right so to do.

Praying in tongues may or may not also be helpful, but they need not be deemed necessity. Sometimes it can be more helpful for the storyteller to hear and understand the prayer that is being offered. However, if the listener has such a gift and feels moved to use it quietly and circumspectly, then it would be right so to do.

The following is an outline of the various kinds of prayer which can be offered in ministry. Each section gives an indication of when it would be appropriate to use it if prompted by the Spirit.

1. Prayers of Thanksgiving

> *Give thanks to the Lord because he is good. His love is eternal.*
>
> Psalm 107: 1

At the conclusion of any listening session, giving thanks in prayer can be a proper starting point for ministry. It can open the storyteller to the influence of the Holy Spirit at work. An initial prayer could include giving thanks for the following.

- The compassion, understanding, mercy, and kindness of God and the presence of the risen Christ Jesus with them now

- The storyteller's courage and desire to talk about feelings that are deeply personal to them and their lives

- The people, places, and events which matter to them about which they have spoken

- Any fresh insight or awareness that has surfaced and been of help to them

Thanksgiving prayer affirms and consolidates what has been shared between listener and storyteller. In it the storyteller can feel that what they have shared has been appreciated and recognised as something of value and worth. It helps them believe that their special circumstances have not been passed by on the other side.

Having opened themselves up and made themselves vulnerable, storytellers need reassurance. They need to know that the source of their life, God Himself, is One in whom they can have complete confidence and trust. These are vital elements to healing. Giving thanks encourages and stimulates this trust.

2. Prayers of Confession

> *I said, I will confess my transgressions unto the Lord;*
>
> Psalm 32: 5
>
> *Therefore being justified by faith, we have peace with God through our Lord Jesus Christ*
>
> Romans 5: 1

Confession gives storytellers a healing opportunity that enables them to rediscover freedom from any disabling guilt. It can deal with regret or a sense of failure that robs the storyteller of peace. Through this particular prayer, storytellers can, perhaps for the first time, openly admit to the sins they feel they have committed.

Freedom to confess without fear, to openly admit without pretence or self-justification, is a hugely healing release. Listeners enable this when they allow storytellers to confess what they have done or said or been without fear of recrimination or judgement.

It is possible that listeners may not believe the things being confessed are sinful. However, if the storyteller believes he or she needs forgiveness, then that is what matters. Listeners will not help storytellers by saying to them, "You needn't feel guilty" or "You shouldn't feel like that" if they most definitely do feel that way! Storytellers need to experience the power of forgiveness in the way that released the paralysed man referred to earlier.

To allow this renewing and releasing experience of forgiveness to take effect, it can be worthwhile asking them to jot down their perceived sins in note form or to dictate them to the listeners for writing down if that is more appropriate. This act can ensure that any confession is not superficial or just something storytellers think the listener, God, or their sources of judgement ought to hear. When such a list is completed, it can be helpful if the listener invites the storyteller to hold the list praying the words "Father, forgive me" or "Lord, have mercy upon me." The list can then be burned in the storyteller's presence. Through this symbolic act they can see their confessed sins being dealt with once and for all with powerful healing affect.

A further step in this confessional process could be for the storyteller to again write down the people or groups against whom he or she has harboured any resentment, bitterness, hatred, or grudge—in other words, the names of people whom the storyteller feels has sinned against him or her. This list could include not just people but anything they blame for hurting, robbing, or depriving them at any time in their lives, things like "bad luck", "chance", "life", or even God Himself.

Listeners can then ask storytellers if they are willing to forgive those who have hurt them. Words like "Father, forgive them (or him or her or it)" can be helpful to use. It might not be easy for the storyteller to do this, but it will help effect their release from any unforgiving spirit or emotion within them. Again, any written list could be destroyed in front of them to emphasise a new way forward.

For any confession to implant a clear sense of forgiveness within storytellers, they need to hear for themselves the words "You are forgiven" not just in a general way, but for specific sins, regrets, or bitter resentments mentioned in their story. Here words of scripture that relate to absolution and forgiveness can be helpful. There needs to be no suggestion of forgiveness being conditional. This would again rob storytellers of the assurance that is required for a return to wholeness. They need to accept forgiveness for that healing renewal. "I receive forgiveness" could be words the listener encourages the storytellers to say as a means of affirming what has taken place.

In the case of the paralysed man recorded in the Gospels, it was a deep-seated knowledge that he was forgiven that enabled the healing to take place. Similarly, it is this knowledge brought about through the prayer process described above that will enable the storyteller to take up his or her bed and walk, free from the paralysis of guilt.

To help re-enforce this absolution, it might be appropriate at this point for listeners to anoint storytellers as a sacramental sign and physical expression of their forgiveness and a new beginning.

3. Prayers of Petition

> *Ask and you will receive; seek and you will find; knock and the door will be opened to you.*
>
> Matthew 7: 7

"What do you want me to do for you?" This was the healing question Jesus addressed to Bartimaeus, a blind beggar at the roadside in Jericho. It encouraged that particular roadside man to identify his own priorities. It clarified in his own mind what he wanted to happen. It enabled him to work out what he felt was needed for a return to wholeness in his life. It was a question where the process of answering helped the process of healing take place. Bartimaeus had no problems in answering. He knew his own heart and desire and was quite ready to call out unashamedly, "I want to see again!"

Sorting out feelings and basic desires is always part of a storyteller's need. Confused hearts and minds create a restless disturbing spirit within. It is part of the listener's role to help storytellers discover what matters most to them. This helps the perplexed thinker clarify which feelings and emotions are robbing him or her of inner peace and well-being. This healing self-discovery can be affected powerfully through prayers of petition.

To enable this kind of prayer to be effective, listeners can invite storytellers to specify if they can what it is they are seeking. What would they like to happen to make things better? From what negative feelings would they like to be released? What changes to the situations, circumstances, people, places, or events referred to in their story would they like to see take place? In other words, "In a perfect world what would you want to happen?" This kind of questioning helps storytellers to reflect much more deeply about their own desires. It enables them to answer for themselves the divine question "What do you want me to do for you?"

When they have begun to sort out their priorities, they can then be encouraged to offer them up as prayers of petition. They can put into clear words what they are asking for. It will be part of the healing process that, through this kind of prayer, storytellers may for the first time be given permission to ask for what they want. It may be that they have come from a background where to ask for anything for themselves was always frowned upon. They were never allowed or encouraged to have this freedom of choice. Inviting them to ask now will make a considerable contribution to the renewal of their self-confidence. It will help release them to go on asking as they continue to sort out their priorities for a renewed life.

"Talk to Jesus" can be a helpful encouragement to some storytellers. It can invite them to make their requests and formulate their own petitions to God. This ensures that it is not the listener who is doing the praying and imposing what he or she feels the other should need or be asking for. By prompting storytellers to ask—and to go on asking—the listener helps them regain confidence in the possibility of ways forward out of the confusion or hopeless despair which they feel they have experienced.

4. Prayers of Intercession

> *I removed his shoulder from the burden: his hands were delivered from the pots.*
>
> Psalm 81: 6

Along with the healing act of asking or petition, healing prayers of intercession can also be part of the renewing ministry. Such prayers can be helpful because they become a means by which storytellers can "hand over" to God the burdens mentioned in their story that are causing them debilitating anxiety or stress.

There is a difference between caring *for* another and caring *about* another. Caring for another can be a practical necessity. Caring about another—feeling somehow responsible for how they feel, how they are, what they might become—can become a burden.

Burdens, of course, will vary according to the circumstances and experiences of the storyteller. They can be people for whom the storyteller feels a heavy, restricting concern. They can be a sick or dependent relative, or their parents, or their children. Even someone who has died can be a burden if the storyteller has not yet properly let go of that person. There can be burdens of duties which storytellers feel they must carry out. There can even be burdens related to faith, when storytellers feel they must achieve exacting standards when high expectations have been laid upon them.

Storytellers will often need permission to hand over things or people they have identified as burdens. They can feel guilty about letting go. They can be fearful about giving them over, feeling that they and they alone are responsible for someone's well-being or a given situation with which they are involved.

Sometimes they don't want to be released, because the burden gratifies an emotional need to be wanted. "If I don't do it, nobody else will" can often be a plaintive cry. One response to that can be "Nobody can do it if you won't let go!" Pride can sometimes come in the disguise of care or service. If this is detected by a discerning listener, it would be right to explore why the storyteller has such a need to be needed.

Having carried something or someone for what may have been many years, it is not always easy to entrust them to another. The storyteller may need help in developing a fresh depth of trust in God. A devoted grandmother was constantly worried about her grandchildren. They were well cared for in a loving home, yet the grandmother was anxious for them in a world she saw as dangerous and insecure for growing children. "I pray for them diligently every night," she declared fervently.

"Would you like to hand them over and every night thank God for doing for them what you cannot possibly do with all your worry or anxiety?" suggested the listener in a time of ministry. The grandmother saw the point. There is a fine line between caring for others and feeling responsible for them, between trusting God with loved ones and not trusting.

Having handed over situations or individuals in prayers of intercession, the storyteller then needs to be exhorted by the listener to leave these things alone and not take them back again. In other words, he or she needs to be encouraged to "let go, and let God." You don't plant bulbs and then keep on digging them up to see if they are growing!

This encouragement can be emphasised by *cutting off* the storyteller from whatever it is they need releasing from. This is a ministry that is particularly relevant when you are dealing with bonds that have enslaved the storyteller in a restrictive or burdensome way. The listener in prayer can say to the storyteller, quite deliberately and with authority, "I take the sword of the Spirit and cut you free from . . ." whatever person, place, practice, or other bondage the storyteller is tied to. This powerful prayer is based on an understanding that Christ seeks to set people free from those things that enslave them.

It can be helpful to remind the storyteller that this cutting off is the equivalent of major medical surgery. It is *spiritual surgery*. Like any surgery, time should be taken to recover. When a leg is amputated, the amputee can still feel their toes for many weeks afterwards. So with a spiritual cutting off, the storyteller needs to give thanks for the letting go and for what God has done, even if initially he or she feels no different.

5. Anointing

> *Is any sick among you? Let him call for the elders of the church; and let them pray over him, anointing him with oil in the name of the Lord: And the prayer of faith shall save the sick, and the Lord shall raise him up; and if he have committed sins, they shall be forgiven him.*
>
> James 5: 14-15

Anointing is a well-documented ministry, a sacramental act which has a depth of history and emphasis in different parts of the church. In recent years it has moved from being a rite for the dead and dying to being a rite for healing and renewal. Through this sacramental act there are again links with the ministry of the Good

Samaritan. He poured oil on the wounds of the half-dead man for healing. In terms of a listening ministry, it is a wonderful and renewing resource available to listeners in their work.

Biblically we can identify up to seven reasons for anointing.

- An act of *rededication* of a life to God for a new beginning

- An act of *re-consecration*, helpful if your storyteller has had experiences of physical defilement through abuse, illness, or disease

- An act of *restoration*, cleansing and purifying body, mind, and spirit

- An act of *redemption*, providing a seal of protection against occult influences or false accusations

- An act of *refreshment*, a sign of the Holy Spirit deepening faith

- An act of *reassurance* in God's authority and his rule over the storyteller's life

Listening is Healing

- An act of *rejoicing*, stimulating a lightening of the spirit when crippling self-doubt or despair has taken over

It is an act which finds best use related to confession and absolution, when there is a desire on the part of the storyteller to be released from guilt or shame. It is also appropriate when deep hurt has been revealed, coupled with prayers of petition or intercession, or when turning away from any occult involvement. In the latter situation, anointing becomes a sign and seal of belonging again to God, a relationship which was deemed to be broken when they committed "spiritual adultery" by turning to other sources for worship, guidance, help, or support. The relationship restored, in turn restores a sense of renewed well-being and self-worth.

Depending on the denominational church order to which the listeners relate, and the position they themselves hold within their church order, it may be necessary for listeners to share this ministry with a priest, minister, or other ordained church leader. Listeners should have no hesitation in calling for such help. If they feel this particular ministry is appropriate to their storyteller's search for wholeness and restoration, then it would be right. In many Anglican traditions the oil to be used will have been blessed by a bishop on Maundy Thursday and will be held by the priest. In other traditions, the oil may be ordinary olive oil which has been prayed over by the listener for this special act. Usually the person ministering the anointing places his or her thumb into the oil and then makes a sign of the cross on the forehead of the recipient with an appropriate prayer, such as: "I anoint you in the name of the Father, the Son, and the Holy Spirit, and may the healing mercies of the risen Lord flow deep within you."

When to anoint will again be a matter of being open to the prompting of the Spirit as the listener remains sensitive to His leading.

6. Sacrament of Communion

> *For I have received of the Lord that which also I delivered unto you, That the Lord Jesus the same night in which he was betrayed took bread: And when he had given thanks, he brake it, and said, Take eat, this is my body, which is broken for you: this do in remembrance of me. After the same manner also he took the cup, when he had supped saying, This cup is the new testament in my blood: this do ye, as oft as ye drink it, in remembrance of me.*
>
> I Corinthians 11: 23-25

The sacrament of communion is something else that can be linked to the parable of the Good Samaritan. He used wine to cleanse and renew and, no doubt, simply to refresh the broken man at the roadside. This particular act of ministry, although it now has a wide variety of theological and ecclesiastical practices and interpretations, can nevertheless be recognised as a supreme healing act. It is an important part of any listening ministry.

Communion may be offered to the storyteller for several reasons. Seen in the light of another healing parable, the Prodigal Son, the son returns home to receive the fatted calf banquet from a loving, rejoicing, accepting, and forgiving parent. This could be an experience with which storytellers need to identify. If their own story has been one of rejection, lost ways, or perceived disobediences, they need to be welcomed back. In these circumstances and following a desire to commit to a new way of life, receiving communion could be a ministry that redeems much of their broken self-worth and sense of unworthy isolation.

Offering the sacrament of communion is not something for every listening occasion, but rather at special times when the storyteller has reached a special point in his or her journey back to wholeness. It could be offered to help the storyteller have a renewed sense of belonging, of being a part of something bigger than his or her own human story of failing or weakness. Sharing the sacrament in the company of others echoes the broken man at the roadside being taken by the Good Samaritan to an inn, where implied fellowship and friendship would have played their part in restoring the hurt person back to a new wholeness and confidence in himself, in others, and in his God.

Again, it may be necessary for the listener to enlist the help of a priest or minister in this piece of ministry. Again, that should not deter the listener from making use of this healing and renewing blessing.

7. Healing of Memories

> *O LORD, thou hast searched me, and known me. Thou knowest my down sitting and mine uprising, thou understand my thought afar off. Thou compassest my path and my lying down, and art acquainted with all my ways.*
>
> Psalm 139: 1-3

This aspect of ministry is well documented and is related to the healing ministry. It is mentioned in outline here as an important part of the listener's response to events shared by the storyteller.

The healing of memories takes place through Christ-centred meditation. Listeners lead the storyteller through a meditative act. The storytellers are gently encouraged to recall some particular event or experience which they previously related in their own story, especially those connected with times of deep hurt.

Bob's story is an example. He spoke of a fearful event that had taken place when he was a small boy out walking in the local park. He had been attacked by a dog. It had rushed at him, jumped up, and tried to bite his face. He was terrified. Ever since then into adulthood, he could not go to that park. Every time he saw a dog, even on film or television, fear welled up inside. He had learned to live with this, but he knew it had spoilt his life.

When he told this story, his listener invited him to recall in his mind's eye the circumstances of that fearful event. With some hesitancy he went back in his imagination to that day in the park. At that point his listener encouraged him to

Listening is Healing

envisage Jesus within the recalled scene. As Bob complied, his listener gently prompted him with the questions, "What is Jesus doing? What can you see?"

Bob's response was immediate. "Jesus is standing in front of me, and the dog has jumped up at him not me. I'm okay."

That ministry experience stayed with Bob, and as time went by the fear loosened its hold on him as he remembered what he had seen. He even returned to walk in the park.

This use of God-given Spirit-led imagination encourages the storyteller to relive the experience with a new perspective. They begin to see the hurtful event with the love and authority of Jesus present at their side. He is sensitive to what they were undergoing. This new picture can redeem the memory and restore it to one that has no further damaging power over them or their emotions.

Quite reasonably, the storyteller or sceptic might ask why Jesus didn't prevent the event from happening in the first place. This is never easy to answer. It has much to do with freewill being part of God's gift to us and our freedom to make choices about what we do and where we go. Scepticism is best replaced with thanksgiving and trust.

This spiritual Christ-centred meditation can be an essential part of storytellers' journey back to wholeness. Through it they are given the opportunity to face experiences that robbed them of peace. Through the healing of memories there is the possibility of a return to wholeness, which the storyteller perhaps believed would never have been possible again.

The healing of memories is the work of the Holy Spirit, revealing truth and ransoming emotion. Listeners become the instruments through which this spiritual healing surgery takes place. It is a ministry in which listeners should have a confidence, because it is a ministry the Holy Spirit seeks for them to employ in appropriate ways and times.

8. Healing the Family Tree

> *Remember ye not the former things, neither consider the things of old. Behold, I will do a new thing; now it shall spring forth; shall ye not know it? I will even make a way in the wilderness, and rivers in the desert.*
>
> Isaiah 43: 16

The purpose of praying for a cleansing of a storyteller's family tree can be to ensure that individuals are set free from any past influences from their family line that might be affecting their lives in the present.

It is not unknown for families, perhaps many years in the past, to have been cursed. Nor is it unheard of that deaths within the family history were never properly dealt with. This was particularly true until quite recently, when a still-born or a miscarriage was not seen as something that required any kind of final rite of passage such as a funeral. Mary was a woman in her late fifties, clearly burdened within. She spoke of having miscarried when she was fifteen years old. It had been an unwanted pregnancy, kept hidden from all but her parents. They gave little support, and neither did the young boy with whom she had intercourse. It was a sordid time, and was never mentioned again. She had felt the child growing within her to be a genuine life. She had even named the unborn to herself and had lived with the guilty and grieving memory of it for over forty years. In response to the story, the listener read to the woman words from Psalm 139. "When my bones were being formed, carefully put together in my mother's womb, when I was growing there in secret, you knew I was there." Mary recognised that her child was known to God. She was prompted to give thanks and hand him over by name to God in prayer, asking that he might now rest in peace in God's love and care. Following this ministry, Mary gradually found a new freedom and a release in the days that followed that she had not known for years. Those who knew her recognised this without ever knowing the cause.

Storytellers may themselves be able to recall and recount a family history or a pattern existing from one generation to the next, such as a line of suicide, miscarriage, repeated illness, disease.

Listening is Healing

One way of addressing these things is to invite the storyteller to use a formal prayer litany as a tool for healing such as the following.

- Father, I offer to you my family tree, my ancestors known and unknown.

- I am sorry for any quarrels or feuds, resentments or grudges, any breaks in fellowship, cruelty of any kind in our family line.

- I renounce any occult involvement in spiritualism, witchcraft, or any religious activity less than Christ-like in our family line.

- I am sorry for any deliberate rejection of Jesus Christ, any underhand dealings, any resort to crime, murder, or immorality of any kind in our family line.

- I commit to you the souls of any suicides, miscarriages, abortions, and still-born children in our family line.

- Father, I thank you that all these negative things are being washed away by the cleansing power of your Holy Spirit. In

> the name of Jesus, our risen Lord and Saviour, Amen.

We are dealing here with mystery. We are affirming our belief that nothing is unknown to God, who is the same yesterday, today, and tomorrow. Encouraging storytellers to offer this prayer aloud, slowly, one section at a time enables them to acknowledge God's sovereignty and rule over the past generations. Any unrecognised fault within their family line is therefore being addressed and ministered to through this prayer of faith and petition. It is like clearing out the cellar so that nothing in the house can be tarnished by its smell or harmful content.

9. Exorcism or Deliverance

> *But deliver us from evil . . .*
>
> Matthew 6: 13

As we have seen in other areas of listening ministry, what the listener believes must not detract in any way from what the storyteller believes. Listeners have no need or right to be cynical, fearful, or over-enthusiastic about this part of ministry. What is needed is a balanced and perceptive approach to matters related to the occult in all its forms.

The storyteller may be *oppressed* by occult involvement but not necessarily *possessed* by evil. Normally, by confessing to any spiritual adultery, they will be enabled to move away from any detrimental effects it may have had. Even if they took part in ignorance, resolving never to indulge again would bring renewal.

This renouncing of spiritual adultery and resolving to walk in the light is an entirely appropriate piece of ministry which listeners could encourage. They could persuade storytellers never to read their horoscope again or to get rid of any lucky charms. They could prompt them to ask for forgiveness for such adultery. They could invite them to declare they will walk faithfully with their God from now on.

Should listeners sense, after checking assumptions and bringing discernment to bear, that demonic possession could be in evidence, that would be the time to seek experienced expertise. It would be right to check with those authorised to deal with such matters. The listeners should have made themselves aware of this resource beforehand. It is a ministry that needs to be carried out by those who are properly qualified. It is not something in which the well-meaning, self-appointed amateur dabbles. Exorcism, despite its glamorisation by film and media, is a genuine and authentic ministry, authorised by the church of Jesus Christ, but it should only take place when and if necessary.

It will only be on rare occasions that this form of ministry will be required. Storytellers may well be influenced by the occult, but few will require such extreme spiritual surgery. In fact, listeners would be doing storytellers no favours if every experience talked about were associated with satanic or demonic involvement that required exorcism.

Suffice it to say that this ministry is available and can be an essential prerequisite to any return to well-being or wholeness. It is a ministry about which listeners should be aware, even if it is wise to leave its particular gifts and expertise to others.

10. Using the Bible

*Thy word is a lamp unto my feet, and
a light unto my path.*

Psalm 119.105

Appropriate texts and passages of scriptures are a powerful tool which listeners have at their disposal. These can be offered to storytellers following listening sessions or at the conclusion of ministry.

The right words of scripture can become a source of renewed inspiration to the storyteller. They can directly speak to his or her experiences and situations. They can be texts which hold out promise, hope, possibilities, and words of reassurance to recall at a later time.

Listeners quote texts or passages so that storytellers might hear helpful and healing words, appropriate to whom they are and where they've been in their life experiences. Sandy had been emotionally and sexually involved with a married man. He had walked away from her, and she came to tell her story. She was guilty. She felt she had let herself down and deeply regretted the short affair. She thought her Christian life was no longer of worth or value. In ministry she confessed her mistake and weakness and asked forgiveness, but she still could not believe herself worthy to be taken back into God's favour. The listener sensitive to her struggle, invited her to hear the words from Romans 8, *For I am persuaded, that neither death, nor life, nor angels, nor principalities, nor powers, nor things present, nor things to come, nor height, nor depth, nor any other creature, shall be able to separate us from the love of God, which is in Christ Jesus our Lord.* The listener read it a second time, and Sandy broke down in tears. Only then was she able to give thanks for what she had now heard applying specifically to her. She was encouraged to take the text home with her and read it whenever she was in doubt about her self-worth or value.

Listeners must take care in case misuse or abuse of Bible texts was part of storytellers' root problems in the first place. It could be that distorted interpretations of selective texts were used as weapons against them in the past. Perhaps indiscriminate texts had hurt, condemned, belittled, or made them feel unclean or unacceptable in some way. They may have been subjected to religious bigotry or narrow prejudice. This is not an uncommon experience if the storyteller has belonged to or been influenced by some fundamentalist group or sect. In such a situation the Bible would have to be offered as a healing agent with a great deal of sensitivity and discretion. The listener would have to be certain that the time was right for biblical quotes to be introduced.

Quoting texts is not something the listener necessarily carries out because of what *they* believe about the power or authority of scripture, or because they have a list of favourite texts. Listeners quote them so that the storytellers might hear helpful and healing words, appropriate to who they are and where they have been in their life experiences. A young woman relayed her story of disillusionment, hurt, and cynicism over the breakdown of her marriage. She was angry, resentful, and bitter at life and at God. As the listener heard her, Psalm 13 came to mind, and she asked if the woman would mind her reading it, saying, "I feel this could have been written just for you."

The storyteller made no objection, so the listener read aloud. *How long wilt thou forget me, O Lord for ever? How long wilt thou hide thy face from me? How long shall I take counsel in my soul, having sorrow in my heart daily? How long shall mine enemy be exalted over me? Consider and hear me, O Lord my God: lighten mine eyes, lest I sleep the sleep of death.* As the woman heard the words she broke down and sobbed, "*That's me! That's me!*" This breakdown, giving in to her need rather than her bitterness, enabled the remainder of the ministry to gently build her up. The beginnings of some hope could once again be restored to her life.

Effective listeners need to be familiar with biblical material suitable for this kind of ministry. They need to draw on a knowledge of texts and passages which can best be offered for healing and wholeness. The listeners need to know their Bible, not as a law book, but as a healing resource through which God can speak to the storyteller. The Psalms are a particularly deep well of healing words and passages. They

Listening is Healing

cover so much of human emotion, feelings, and struggles with belief and faith. The good listener will be able to draw on their healing waters on many occasions.

It might well be that some of the texts found in the contents of this book could properly be offered in ministry. An appropriate word can be given directly to those seeking release and renewal.

If an appropriate text or passage does come to the listener's mind, then it would be helpful to jot down the book, chapter, and verse reference to give to the storyteller to take away. This would be a constant reminder of what God did for them in that special time of ministry.

11. Social, Medical, and Practical Ministry

> *He maketh me to lie down in green pastures: he leadeth me beside the still waters. He restoreth my soul:*
>
> Psalm 23: 2-3

(i) Social Ministry

In looking at the kind of ministry listeners might offer we have emphasised *spiritual ministry* such as prayer and sacrament. There are, however, other things that listeners may wish to do in response to the storyteller's need for a return to wholeness.

The Good Samaritan offered more than oil, wine, and bandages. He also took the broken man to an inn where others became involved in the healing process. There was the innkeeper, the people in the inn, and by implication, food, drink, and probably a decent bed. All this points to the fact, that *social ministry* may also be required for a storyteller's healing.

Some storytellers may need to be released from some particularly destructive or negative social

Listening is Healing

environment. Maybe they have been caught up in a difficult or abusive family situation. Perhaps they carry heavy work responsibility with seemingly no opportunity for time off. They could simply be weighed down with care. It may be a listener's ministry to help the storyteller *stop doing* and *start being*. They may need practical help to get away from their situations for some respite care.

Listeners should make themselves aware of possible *inns of healing*, places where storytellers can go to find rest, rediscover their own selfhood, and take fresh stock of priorities. They may need to be encouraged to let go of responsibilities for a time so they can address their own well-being.

Part of the listener's ministry might be to ensure the storyteller is put in touch with people or communities whose relationships can encourage him or her into a new life. It might even be right to arrange for the storyteller to be introduced to an acceptable and caring befriender or caring agency. Whatever seems right, the principle here is to ensure that the storytellers have a supportive and healing community around them to restore any sense of isolation or burden which has overwhelmed them.

(ii) Medical Ministry

Honour a physician with the honour due unto him for the uses which ye may have of him: for the Lord hath created him.

Apocrypha Ben Sira 38 (KJV)

In the case of some storytellers, it may be that what is required for healing is to help them face the realities of a physical condition. They may need to be prompted to seek proper medical attention. Rightly, the listener might pray for physical healing, but healing for the storyteller could be to visit a doctor to receive specific medical attention. A balanced listening ministry does not discredit or ignore medical insight and help. Believing in the power of prayer and the healing touch of Christ does not exclude medical care.

Some storytellers may be afraid to seek medical help. They may fear finding out that something is not right them or that they may have contracted some disease. They could have some misguided belief related to medicine, thinking it to be not of God. They could be too proud to admit need. It will be up to the listeners to discern what the issue here is and encourage the storyteller to refer to a doctor if necessary.

"Do you want to be well?" This was a question Jesus asked a man by a pool. The local superstition was that if you were the first into the water in the pool when it bubbled up, you would be cured. The man complained he had nobody to help him get into the water despite having been there for thirty-eight years. Quite rightly, Jesus saw this as a somewhat flimsy excuse—hence the challenging question, "Do you want to be well?" Sometimes it is a question worth asking a sickly storyteller who resists opportunities for healing. Their response can indicate their level of desire to be well and whole.

Sometimes being ill may seem preferable to being well. Illness can mean freedom from responsibility. No one wants pain or suffering, but as in the case of a child not wishing to attend school, it can always be helpful to have a slight tummy upset in the morning prior to going. It can also be a means of gaining sympathetic attention. It could be that as a child the storyteller only received attention or affection when he or she was ill. Illness became a necessary means to achieve notice.

In adulthood these same patterns can persist. John was never a well man, but doctors could find nothing wrong with him. Eventually, in a time of prayer ministry, he admitted he was afraid his wife would leave him if he was well and she had no need to care for him. The issue was not his health but his fear of rejection. Listeners need to be aware of these traits in order to ensure that any kind of ministry they offer to the storyteller is directed at the root of the problem.

(iii) Practical Ministry

For as the body without the spirit is dead, so faith without works is dead also.

James 2: 26

It would be blind folly to offer storytellers prayer, sacrament, deliverance, retreats, or pills, only to discover that what was actually needed for healing was someone to fix their heating, mend their cars, or baby-sit poorly children so the anxious parents could go back to work and earn some income! However, listeners need to guard against taking personal responsibility for the practical well-being of every storyteller they encounter.

To cover this category of ministry, caring listeners should make themselves aware of specialised resources available—agencies to whom storytellers could turn for practical help and people who could provide financial expertise or offer appropriate legal advice.

The Samaritan in the Good Samaritan parable made sure that the practicalities were taken care of. He knew of an innkeeper. He gave him money to ensure whatever was needed for healing would be paid for. This analogy, of course, should not be stretched beyond sound judgement. A golden rule of any listening ministry should be to *never give money*! Apart from setting a dangerous precedent that would be hard to maintain, such a gesture will not help heal storytellers' root inability to manage their life's affairs.

If money is required for something specific, such as a ticket for a bus or train, something to eat or drink, or a place to sleep, these things could be supplied from resources listeners are already aware of locally. This would be part of their preparedness for this aspect of healing.

With all their compassion, listeners should resist the temptation to take personal responsibility for meeting practical needs. Rather, they should know where that need might be met elsewhere. In this way they will be able to exercise a practical ministry far more effectively and extensively than otherwise would be possible through relying on their own individual resources.

Chapter Six

At the Conclusion of Ministry

> *Wherefore take unto you the whole armour of God that ye may be able to withstand in the evil day, and having done all, to stand. Stand therefore, having your loins girt about with truth, and having on the breastplate of righteousness; And your feet shod with the preparation of the gospel of peace; Above all, taking the shield of faith, wherewith ye shall be able to quench all the fiery darts of the wicked. And take the helmet of salvation, and the sword of the Spirit, which is the word of God:*
>
> Ephesians 6: 13-18

Following medical surgery, a patient is normally sent home with a list of instructions about how to take care of him—or herself in the days following the treatment. So it is with spiritual surgery and the consequence of intensive prayer ministry. The storyteller can be given a checklist of dos and don'ts to sustain his or her on-going renewal. The list can include the following for guidance.

- Live out your healing by praying constantly with thanksgiving for what God through the ministry of His Spirit has done for you.

- Resist talking to others about what has been shared, but let your changed attitudes and demeanour speak for you.

- Watch out for other people's cynicism about your listening experience. Hold on to what was good for you.

- Regularly recall any words spoken to you from scripture.

- Don't expect others to be different.

- Retrain your mind with truth if that is necessary. For example, remember you are not a failure, unloved, or unforgiven; you are a beloved child of God.

Listening is Healing

- Stay rooted in regular worship, sacrament, and prayer.

- Be open to a need to talk some more.

Appendix: A Way Forward

Which now of these three, thinkest thou, was neighbour unto him that fell among the thieves?

And he said, He that shewed mercy on him.

Then said Jesus unto him, Go and do thou likewise.

Luke 10: 36,37

If what you have read encourages you to consider developing a listening ministry within your own church or perhaps as a group of churches together, how might that be achieved?

First, such a ministry would need to be something agreed by those who already have responsibility for pastoral care within the church. Any listening ministry needs to be seen as a part of what is already there. It needs to be an extension of the care that already exists, not a separate isolated ministry unrelated to the whole.

Having agreed about the need for this ministry and believing it to be part of the work of the Holy Spirit, the next step is to identify those within your church community who might be called to exercise such a ministry.

The way to do this is *not* to ask for volunteers! What is needed is for the church fellowship itself to identify its potential listeners. One way of doing this is to invite every member of the fellowship to submit the names of the people they feel might have the gifts and graces to be good listeners. "Who would you be willing to talk to in confidence?" can be a helpful question for them to address before adding names to any list.

How many names you might be seeking will depend of the size of your fellowship. A congregation of twenty to fifty might be looking for three or four people, fifty to one hundred might feel that seven or eight names could be forthcoming, and over one hundred could be looking for ten or more.

When all the names have been submitted to the pastoral leadership, several will stand out as being repeated by most people. These

Listening is Healing

then could be identified as those called by the congregation. They could gather together to begin a process of exploration of the shape a listening ministry might take within their church or with those from other churches nearby.

The group could then commit themselves to reading this book, for example. Together they could discuss its chapters in a series of reflections. It might also be helpful to invite outside speakers to share in this process of learning.

A further way forward could be to produce an explanatory leaflet for your church or group of churches. It could inform people that a listening service was available for anyone who wished to talk to somebody in complete confidence about any matter whatsoever. People wanting to know more should contact . . . and here you would include an appropriate contact number. This initial contact would ascertain the nature of the request and let them know this was a Christian listening service. If it was appropriate on both sides, two listeners could then be allocated to the enquirer. The listeners would make contact and arrange a time and place for their coming together with the person wishing to talk.

As with any new venture, steps need to be taken slowly, and there should be no pressure of time in seeking to establish such a ministry. The fact that this is a work of the Holy Spirit within the life of the church means prayerfully listening to God. That is the hallmark of those seeking to develop such an undertaking.

The need for listening ears, to give people struggling with their lives some hope, cannot be overstated. The Christ of the first century seeks to minister to the broken and lost of the twenty-first century, but He needs His people to fulfil this love. At the conclusion of the parable of the Good Samaritan, Jesus said, "Go and do the same." His church is called to explore every possible avenue that takes it down that road of care. Listening is healing. Not to engage in it means that those who long for a life ransomed, healed, restored, and forgiven will continue to be passed by on the other side.

The church has been given this mandate to care.

Lightning Source UK Ltd.
Milton Keynes UK
UKOW041600080413

208877UK00001B/4/P